DATE DUE

ABC

for You and Me

ABC

for You and Me

WRITTEN BY **Meg Girnis**

PHOTOGRAPHY BY **Shirley Leamon Green**

Albert Whitman & Company
Chicago, Illinois

Library of Congress Cataloging-in-Publication Data

Girnis, Margaret.

ABC for you and me / by Margaret Girnis;

p. cm.

Summary: Photographs show children with Down syndrome in

activities with objects corresponding to the letters of the alphabet.

ISBN 978-0-8075-0101-6

1. Down syndrome—Juvenile literature. [1. Down syndrome.

2. Mentally handicapped. 3. Alphabet.] I. Title

RJ506.D68 G57 2000

618.92'858842[E]—dc21 99-039072

Designed by Scott Piehl.

To our Heavenly Father and all the wonderful people
He has introduced me to through my daughters,
Amanda and Jaimie. — M. G.

In memory of my sister-in-law
Audrey Green (1945-1985). — S. L. G.

*The author and photographer would like to thank
the Burns, Calleo, Colone, Diaz, Fell-DeWalt,
Hammond, Hampton-Canady, Marrero, Mazza, Rogers,
Schuhle, and Shank families, who took the time to have
their children photographed for this book.*

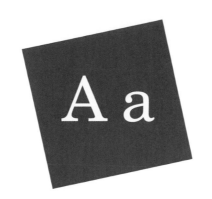

Apple

B b

Ball

C c

Cat

Dog

E e

Elephant

F f

Flowers

G g

Guitar

H h

Hug

Ice cream

J j

Jack-in-the-box

K k

Kite

L l

Leaf

M m

Mirror

N n

Nest

O o

Orange

Pp

Puzzle

Q q

Quilt

Rr

Rabbit

S s

Sand

T t

Tractor

U u

Umbrella

V v

Vacuum cleaner

W w

Wagon

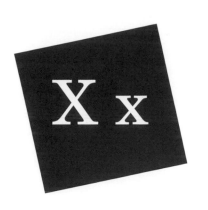

Xylophone

Y y

Yarn

Z z

Zebra